To teachers everywhere
who help make preschool such a special place to be!
Always to Erik, Emma, & Wyatt, with love
—H. M.

To preschoolers everywhere—
happy school days!
—L. R.

What to Expect at Preschool
Text and illustrations copyright © 2001 by Heidi Murkoff
What to Expect Kids® is a registered trademark of Heidi Murkoff.
Growing Up Just Got Easier™ and Angus™ are trademarks of Heidi Murkoff.
HarperCollins®, ♣®, and HarperFestival® are registered trademarks of HarperCollins Publishers Inc.
Printed in the U.S.A. All rights reserved.
Library of Congress catalog card number: 2001087372
www.harperchildrens.com

What to Expect
at Preschool

Heidi Murkoff

Illustrated by Laura Rader

HarperFestival®
A Division of HarperCollinsPublishers

A Word to Parents

It's hard to believe, but your child's starting preschool. Even if it's just for a couple of hours two or three days a week, it seems such a big step for someone in such little sneakers.

How can you prepare yourself and your child for this milestone? How can you help ensure that this first, important stop on his or her academic journey is a happy and successful one?

What to Expect at Preschool is a good place to start. It is designed to answer many of the questions your child may have about preschool, providing just the right amount of information so that your child feels empowered, but not so much that he or she feels overwhelmed.

You'll notice as you read that the questions and the answers in this book are very concrete, offering accurate descriptions of the basic aspects of preschool: what the classroom will look like, what teachers do, what happens in a typical preschool day. This is because young children are very literal, and their concerns about new experiences fundamental, centered on their basic needs (Will I be taken care of? Who will take care of me?). What has been intentionally omitted from this book are projections that might promise more than preschool may realistically be able to deliver: that it will always be fun (there will be times when it won't be), that all the children will always be your friends (some will be, some won't be), that you'll always love school (there will be days that you will and days that you won't).

Supplement the general information about school in this book with some specifics about your child's preschool. After you tour the school yourself, bring back your own descriptions: "I saw an art easel; I saw a block area; I saw lots of puzzles and books; I saw a pet gerbil named Sam. I met your teachers and their names are Miss Sharon and Mrs. Kelly." If the preschool allows it, bring back some snapshots as well. Some schools permit children to visit the classroom before school begins. If yours doesn't, a drive or walk by the building can make the concept of school more tangible. Other schools

organize home visits by teachers, while some hold get-togethers for new students. If your preschool doesn't plan such get-togethers, consider hosting or co-hosting one yourself. It's a great opportunity for parents and children to become familiar with each other before the big day arrives. Encouraging your child to "play" school will also give him or her the chance to practice social skills and work out anxieties. The day before the big day, you might also stage a dress rehearsal, which includes getting completely ready and walking or driving to school.

Whenever possible try to build the concept of ownership into your conversations about school: "This is *your* school; this will be *your* teacher; these will be *your* classmates." Feeling territorial about school helps children feel more in control, more comfortable and secure, so that ultimately they will feel successful about the preschool experience.

Even with all the right preparation, there will still be adjustments to be made once preschool begins. Most preschools start with a phase-in period, which helps parents and children gradually make the transition to a full, parent-free school day. You might explain to your child: "I will be staying with you for a little while at school until you get to know it. When you get to know it, you will stay with the other children and the teachers." When you do leave, keep it short and sweet and without the kind of drama that might inspire fear in your child ("If she's that sad about leaving, this must be a pretty bad place"). Don't sneak out without a good-bye, but do enlist a teacher's help if the separation becomes difficult. And give it time. As with any major transition, your child may take many steps forward and many steps backward in the same week.

For many more tips on helping a child prepare for preschool, read *What to Expect the Toddler Years*. Wishing you a wonderful first day of school.

heidi

All aboard! Join the preschool train!

Just Ask Angus

Hello! My name is Angus. Some people call me the Answer Dog, because I like to answer all kinds of questions about growing up. It's good to ask questions because what you know, helps you grow!

So, I hear you're going to preschool soon. Or maybe you just want to learn about preschool. Either way, I bet you have a lot of questions, and I'm here to answer all of those questions. I'm going to show you and tell you everything you need to know about school: what it looks like, who goes there, what kids do there. That way, when the first day of preschool comes, you'll know what to expect.

Are you ready to find out what to expect at preschool? Then let's get started! Follow me. . . .

Your friend,

Angus

P.S. I've put a little game or idea to think about on the bottom of every page. Look for my paw print, and you'll find it! Have fun!

What's preschool?

Preschool is a place where children go to play and learn and have fun. At preschool, you will be with a group of children your age called a class. Every class has nice grown-ups called teachers who take care of the children. Classes are like your school family—you and your class will spend all your time at preschool together. Your class will have its own special room called a classroom—filled with all the things that make preschool fun and interesting.

What will you take to preschool?

Are you getting ready to go to preschool soon? What's the name of your preschool?

What will my classroom look like?

Your classroom will have tables and chairs that are just your size. It will probably have an area for playing dress-up and house; an area for blocks and trucks; an area for painting, pasting, and coloring; and a quiet area for looking at books. Your classroom may also have a kitchen for making snacks, a big tub for water or rice or sand play, and maybe even a class pet (like a fish or a gerbil). In your classroom you will also have a special place called a cubby to keep all of your important things from home, like your coat and boots and your favorite blanket or teddy bear. You may have your own cubby or share one with a buddy.

Look around your room at home. Do you see some of the same things you'll see in your classroom?

What's a teacher?

A teacher is a very nice grown-up who takes care of children and helps them learn and have fun. Your teachers will set up your classroom every day with activities just for you and your class. They will read to you, sing to you, do art projects with you, play games with you, take walks with you, go to the playground with you, and help you learn the rules that make your preschool a happy and safe place to be. Your teachers will help you when you need help and hug you when you need a hug. They will find out all about you: what you like and don't like, what makes you happy or sad, what makes you special.

What will you teach your class?

You can play preschool at home. You can be the teacher and your dolls or stuffed animals can be the class!

They will read to you...

do art projects with you...

help you learn... and even give you a hug!

Your teacher will find out what makes you special!

Will my mommy or daddy stay with me at preschool?

Your mommy or daddy or babysitter will take you to preschool and pick you up when preschool is over. They may stay for just a little while so you can show them some of the great things there are to do in your classroom. But they can't stay all day, because preschool is for children, not for grown-ups! That's OK, because at the end of the day when they come to pick you up, you can tell them all about the fun you had at preschool.

Preschool is one thing that's just for children. Can you think of any other things?

Where else do you find lots of children?

What will I do at preschool?

Preschool is filled with lots of fun and interesting things to do, so you will always be busy! Most days, your class will have circle time (when everyone sits together in a circle to talk about the day), story time (when the teachers read books to you), music or movement time (when you sing songs or do finger rhymes or dance), art time (when you make a picture or a project to hang up on the wall or take home). There will also be time to play with all the toys in your classroom, time to play outdoors on the playground, time for snack (yum!), and time for clean-up (when the whole class cleans up together). Your class may also have rest time (when you lie down on cots or mats for a nap) and lunchtime (when you eat lunch you've brought from home).

What do you think your favorite time at preschool will be?

I like making music and dancing! What about you?

What happens at circle time?

Circle time is one of the best parts of the preschool day. Can you guess why it's called circle time? Because it's the time when everyone sits in a circle! During circle time many things will happen. First, your teacher will talk about everything your class will do that day. Then she may give out jobs. Having a job means you're the teacher's special helper. Everyone in your class will take turns having jobs, like being the line leader or door holder, passing out snacks, or putting away books. During circle time you may also talk about the class rules, sing a good-morning song, talk about the weather, listen to a story, and have show-and-tell. Show-and-tell is when children show a favorite toy or book or share news about something special from home.

Sharing a favorite toy can be fun at circle time.

What would you like to bring in from home to share with the class?

Why are there special rules at preschool?

Your teacher will set up special rules for your classroom to make things fair, so everyone has more fun. Some of the rules in your class may be raising your hand when you have a question or want to say something during circle time, using your "inside voice" while you're playing inside so everyone can hear each other, taking turns, sharing, talking nicely to each other, using your words instead of hitting or grabbing, and cleaning up after you're done with an activity. When everybody follows the rules, the classroom is a much more fun and safe place to be!

You can practice raising your hand or using your "inside voice."

Raise your hand up high so the teacher can see it.

Who will I play with?

Your class will have lots of boys and girls your age to play with. You may already know some of the children in your class or you may be meeting them for the first time. Either way, you'll get to know them all, play with them all, and make lots of new friends. Some things your whole class will do together, like listening to stories. Some things you'll do with just one or two other children, like playing in the sandbox. And some things you'll do by yourself, like putting together a puzzle. For other activities, like painting at the easel, you'll take turns.

For some activities, you may have a buddy, who is your special partner. You and your buddy may hold hands when your class takes a walk.

You and your buddy make a great team!

What if I get hungry or have to go to the potty? What if I need a hug?

Getting hungry is no problem, because all preschools have snack times and some preschools even have lunch. Going to the potty is no problem either, because all preschools have bathrooms (and the best thing is, the potties and sinks will be just your size!). You can go to the potty anytime you have to—all you have to do is ask your teacher. In fact, you can ask your teacher for help with anything, like tying your shoes, zipping up or buttoning your jacket, or cleaning up a spill. Need a hug? Teachers are great at giving those, too!

What are some things that your parents help you with at home that you may need to ask your teacher to help you with at school?

Your teacher will help you do this at school.

When will I go home?

When preschool is over, it's pick-up time for all the children in your class. Your mommy or daddy or babysitter will come back to take you home. That's a good time to show them some of the things you did in school that day or to have them meet some of the friends you made. It's also the time to take all the things you were keeping in your cubby or box home with you. Maybe you'll take home some pictures you made, too! Then it's the time to say good-bye to all of the other children and to your teachers. See you on the next school day!

You can mark your preschool days on the calendar with stickers.

Some children go to preschool just for the morning or the afternoon, some go two or three days a week, and some go every day. How often will you go to preschool?